CRACKING THE CODE: HONNE AND TATEMAE IN JAPAN

BY

Brian Takahashi

TABLE OF CONTENTS

Introduction 5

Chapter One: What are Honne and Tatemae? Are People lying to me? 7

Chapter Two: The Historical Context of Honne and Tatemae. 11

Chapter Three: Uses and Significance of Honne and Tatemae. 18

Chapter Four: Japanese Concepts That Influence Honne and Tatemae. 23

Chapter Five: Japanese Social Norms Foreign to the West 30

Chapter Six: Cross-Cultural Communication and Practical Application 34

Chapter Seven: Recognizing Honne and Tatemae with Tips and Strategies 42

Conclusion 47

About the Author 48

Introduction

Do you ever feel like there's a hidden layer to communication when interacting with people in Japan? Do you need help understanding the true meaning behind what someone is saying or doing? If so, you're not alone. Welcome to the fascinating world of "honne" and "tatemae."

In Japan, these two concepts are integral to social interaction and communication. Honne refers to a person's true feelings, desires, and intentions. In contrast, tatemae refers to the social facade they present. At first glance, it may seem like a deceptive and confusing way of interacting, but understanding these concepts is crucial to building meaningful relationships in Japan.

Throughout the book, you'll discover the history, cultural implications, and practical applications of honne and tatemae in Japanese society. You'll learn how these concepts originated, how they have evolved, and how they are used in everyday life. You'll also discover the critical role that honne and tatemae play in cross-cultural communication and how to navigate situations where they come into play.

You'll learn the definitions of honne and tatemae, the differences between the two concepts, and how they are used in Japanese society. We'll also cover some common misconceptions about these concepts and provide examples of how they work in practice.

We'll dive into the historical context of honne and tatemae. We'll explore the cultural influences that shaped these concepts and examine how they were used in the past. By understanding the historical context, you'll better appreciate how honne and tatemae are still relevant in modern-day Japan.

Examining examples of honne and tatemae in modern society, you'll learn how these concepts are used today compared to the past and their role in social interactions. You'll also discover how to recognize and respond to honne and tatemae in everyday situations.

Exploring the cultural implications of honne and tatemae, we'll examine how they relate to other artistic concepts, such as face-saving and indirect communication, and the importance of understanding them in cross-cultural communication.

We'll provide practical applications for foreigners interacting with Japanese people. You'll learn tips for recognizing and responding to honne and tatemae and strategies for navigating situations where they come into play. By the end of this chapter, you'll better understand how to communicate effectively with people in Japan.

You'll come away from this ebook with a deeper understanding of honne and tatemae and the skills and knowledge to navigate cross-cultural communication in Japan.

Whether planning a trip to Japan, doing business with Japanese companies, or simply being interested in Japanese culture, understanding honne and tatemae is essential. Let's explore this fascinating world together!

Chapter One: What are Honne and Tatemae? Are People lying to me?

What is Honne and Tatemae:

In Japanese culture, honne and tatemae are crucial concepts for understanding the difference between a person's true feelings and public facade or persona. Honne refers to a person's genuine feelings, desires, and intentions, which they may keep hidden or unexpressed in Japanese society. Honne is considered a person's inner voice or true self, encompassing their private thoughts, opinions, and emotions that they may not reveal to others. Honne can range from positive to negative emotions, depending on the situation and a person's feelings. It is often considered to be a profoundly personal and private matter.

Tatemae, on the other hand, refers to a person's behavior or actions in public, often to conform to social expectations or avoid conflict. Tatemae is the public facade or persona that a person presents to others, which may differ from their honne. Tatemae is considered to be the face that a person shows to society. It can be seen as a way to maintain social harmony, respect for others, and avoid confrontation.

It is common in Japanese culture for people to hide their honne and display tatemae. Tatemae is often seen as a way to maintain social harmony and avoid conflict. However, this can also lead to a need for more communication and understanding between individuals. It understands the difference between honne and tatemae to effectively communicate with others and build meaningful relationships.

honne and tatemae are two crucial concepts in Japanese culture that describe the difference between a person's true feelings and their public facade or persona. Honne refers to a person's genuine feelings or intentions. In contrast, tatemae refers to the behavior or actions they display publicly. Understanding the distinction between honne and tatemae is crucial for effective communication and building meaningful relationships in Japanese culture.

Japanese Collectivism with Honne and Tatemae:

Japanese collectivism is a cultural concept that has deep roots in Japanese society and is essential in shaping social norms, behaviors, and interactions. This artistic concept is reflected in the way Japanese people interact with each other, where it is common to prioritize group needs over individual needs. In Japanese culture, there is a strong emphasis on the importance of the group and the idea of putting the group's needs before one's desires.

This collectivist culture is closely tied to the concepts of honne and tatemae, which are used to maintain social harmony and avoid conflict. Tatemae behavior is the public facade or persona that a person presents to others, often used to maintain social balance and prevent conflict. It is often seen as necessary for the sake of the group or organization, as it helps to maintain a sense of order and unity.

Honne behavior, on the other hand, is a person's true feelings, desires, and intentions, often hidden or unspoken in Japanese society. Honne behavior can be seen as a threat to the group's harmony, as it can lead to conflicts or disagreements. Therefore, individuals are often expected to keep their honne to themselves and instead display tatemae behavior to maintain group harmony.

The emphasis on group harmony and consensus can also lead to a more indirect communication style in Japanese culture. It is common for Japanese people to avoid confrontation or criticism, as this can threaten the group's harmony. Instead, Japanese people may use subtle hints or non-verbal cues to convey their message or avoid hurting someone's feelings. This indirect communication style is closely tied to the cultural concept of tatemae, as it helps to maintain group harmony by avoiding direct conflicts or criticisms.

While Japanese collectivism can have some negative consequences, it is a fundamental part of Japanese society and plays an essential role in shaping social norms and behaviors. The emphasis on group harmony and consensus can lead to a strong sense of obligation and loyalty to the group, reflected in how Japanese people view their work and relationships. For example, it is common for Japanese employees to stay with the same company for their entire career out of a sense of obligation and loyalty to the company and its values.

Group harmony and consensus can also have some negative consequences. For example, it can lead to a lack of creativity or innovation. Individuals may hesitate to express their ideas or challenge the status quo for fear of disrupting group harmony. Additionally, it can lead to a reluctance to ask for help or support, as individuals may feel it is their responsibility to handle things independently.

In navigating Japanese culture, it is essential to understand the concept of honne and tatemae. Understanding these cultural concepts can help to avoid misunderstandings and miscommunications and can also help to build stronger relationships with Japanese colleagues and friends. It is also essential to respect the importance of group harmony in Japanese culture and to recognize the value of loyalty and commitment to the group.

Understanding Honne and Tatemae in Japanese Society:

Japan has a long tradition of collective harmony and conformity, emphasizing social hierarchy and respect for authority. In such a society, expressing one's feelings and opinions openly can be seen as disruptive or disrespectful, particularly towards those in positions of power.

Japanese people often use tatemae, or a public face, to conform to social norms and avoid offending others. For instance, when asked how they are doing, it is customary to respond with "genki desu" (I am fine), even if they may feel quite the opposite. Tatemae reflects the cultural value of "Wa" or harmony, emphasizing the importance of avoiding conflict and maintaining social cohesion.

At the same time, however, there is a strong sense of individualism and personal identity in Japanese society, particularly among younger generations. The concept of honne, or one's true feelings and intentions, reflects this desire for individual expression and authenticity. While honne is often hidden behind tatemae, it is still vital for individuals to express their true feelings and be understood by those close to them.

The tension between honne and tatemae can create challenges for communication in Japanese society. For example, a foreigner might interpret a Japanese person's tatemae as insincere or superficial, leading to misunderstandings or mistrust. Likewise, a Japanese person might feel uncomfortable expressing their honne to someone outside their close circle, which could be seen as breaking social norms.

In navigating this complexity, it is crucial to understand the context in which honne and tatemae are used. Generally, tatemae is more likely to be used in formal or public settings, such as in the workplace or with strangers. Honne, on the other hand, is more likely to be expressed in informal or private environments, such as with close friends or family.

It is essential to pay attention to nonverbal cues, as these can often convey a person's true feelings even when their words do not. For example, a Japanese person might avoid eye contact or use a more indirect tone when expressing their honne, indicating that they share something personal or sensitive.

Understanding honne and tatemae can be particularly important for building trust and developing relationships in business settings. For instance, a foreign businessperson might need to know the difference between what their Japanese counterpart is saying (tatemae) and what they mean (honne) to make effective decisions and negotiate successfully. Conversely, a Japanese businessperson might need to be aware of how their tatemae is perceived by their foreign counterparts to avoid misunderstandings or miscommunications.

Beyond communication, honne and tatemae have broader cultural implications in Japanese society. For example, using tatemae can sometimes lead to a lack of transparency or accountability in specific contexts, such as government or business. In recent years, there has been a growing awareness of the need to balance tatemae with more honest and direct communication to promote greater trust and openness.

Chapter Two: The Historical Context of Honne and Tatemae.

Honne and Tatemae are Old, Very Old:

One of Japan's earliest examples of honne and tatemae can be traced back to the Heian period (794-1185). During this time, the aristocracy placed great importance on appearances and social status. Women were expected to act in a certain way in public, which often involved concealing their true thoughts and feelings. Hiding your thoughts was particularly true of court ladies, who were always expected to exhibit grace and poise. As a result, tatemae became an essential aspect of courtly etiquette, and women were taught to present themselves in a particular manner to maintain their social standing.

The concept of honne and tatemae continued to evolve throughout Japanese history. During the Edo period (1603-1868), social status became even more critical, and people were expected to behave in a way that was appropriate to their rank. Samurai, for example, were expected to be stoic and brave, even in the face of danger or adversity. This stoicism often required them to suppress their genuine emotions and present a façade of strength and courage, known as tatemae.

Honne remained an important concept, particularly in personal relationships. Samurai were expected to be honest and loyal to their lords and families. This honesty and loyalty often meant expressing their true feelings, even if it meant going against social norms or risking their own lives. This duality of honne and tatemae was reflected in many aspects of samurai culture, including their poetry, art, and philosophy.

During the Meiji period (1868-1912), Japan underwent a period of modernization and Westernization. The concepts of honne and tatemae were still prevalent, but they took on new meanings in the rapidly changing society. Tatemae became associated with modernization and progress, while honne was considered a traditional and somewhat outdated concept. The emphasis on tatemae led to a greater focus on outward appearances and a desire to conform to Western standards of behavior and etiquette.

In the years leading up to World War II, the Japanese government used the concept of tatemae to promote nationalistic and militaristic ideas. Citizens were expected to present a unified front and suppress dissenting opinions or feelings. Honne was seen as a potential threat to the social order, and those who expressed their true thoughts or feelings were often punished or ostracized.

After the war, Japan underwent a period of reflection and re-evaluation. The concept of honne and tatemae came under scrutiny, and many people began to question the role of tatemae in society. Some argued that tatemae had become a tool of oppression to suppress individuality and stifle dissent. Others maintained that tatemae was essential to Japanese culture and helped maintain social harmony and cohesion.

Today, the concepts of honne and tatemae play an essential role in Japanese society. While the emphasis on tatemae has diminished somewhat, it remains a crucial aspect of social interaction and communication. Many Japanese people still feel that presenting a confident face to the world is vital, particularly in formal or professional settings. At the same time, however, the importance of honne has also been recognized, and people are encouraged to express their true thoughts and feelings in personal relationships and more informal settings.

The "Wa" of Japan:

In Japanese culture, the "和" or "Wa" concept is highly valued and crucial in social dynamics and communication. Wa refers to harmony, balance, and peaceful coexistence, and it is often used to describe the ideal state of relationships between people, groups, and even nature. Understanding Wa is essential for anyone seeking to interact with Japanese society on a deeper level, whether for business, personal relationships, or cultural exploration.

Wa is deeply rooted in Japanese history and cultural values. Japan has a long tradition of collective harmony and conformity, emphasizing social hierarchy and respect for authority. In such a society, expressing one's feelings and opinions openly can be seen as disruptive or disrespectful, particularly towards those in positions of power. As a result, Japanese people often use tatemae, or a public face, to conform to social norms and avoid offending others. Tatemae reflects the cultural value of Wa, which emphasizes the importance of preventing conflict and maintaining social cohesion.

At the same time, however, there is a strong sense of individualism and personal identity in Japanese society, particularly among younger generations. The concept of honne, or one's true feelings and intentions, reflects this desire for individual expression and authenticity. While honne is often hidden behind tatemae, it is still crucial for individuals to express their true feelings and be understood by those close to them.

The tension between honne and tatemae can create challenges for communication in Japanese society. While navigating this complexity, it is essential to understand the context in which honne and tatemae are used. Generally, tatemae is more likely to be used in formal or public settings, such as in the workplace or with strangers. Honne, on the other hand, is more likely to be expressed in informal or private environments, such as with close friends or family.

It is essential to pay attention to nonverbal cues, as these can often convey a person's true feelings even when their words do not. For example, a Japanese person might avoid eye contact or use a more indirect tone when expressing their honne, indicating that they share something personal or sensitive.

Understanding Wa can be significant for building trust and developing relationships in business settings. For instance, a foreign businessperson might need to know the difference between what their Japanese counterpart is saying (tatemae) and what they mean (honne) to make effective decisions and negotiate successfully. Conversely, a Japanese businessperson might need to be aware of how their tatemae is perceived by their foreign counterparts to avoid misunderstandings or miscommunications.

Beyond communication, Wa has broader cultural implications in Japanese society. For example, using tatemae can sometimes lead to a lack of transparency or accountability in specific contexts, such as government or business. In recent years, there has been a growing awareness of the need to balance tatemae with more honest and direct communication to promote greater trust and openness.

Likewise, the pressure to conform to social norms and maintain Wa can sometimes lead to a reluctance to challenge authority or speak out against injustice. This reluctance has been evident in Japan's history of political and social movements, where the emphasis on harmony and conformity has often been at odds with the desire for social change and progress.

Understanding Wa is crucial for anyone seeking to navigate the complexities of Japanese society and culture. It requires a nuanced understanding of the balance between individual expression and social harmony and an awareness of the context and nonverbal cues that underlie communication. With this knowledge, one can build deeper relationships, communicate more effectively, and navigate cultural differences more easily.

How Honne and Tatemae are Different in the Modern Era:

One of the most significant differences in the use of honne and tatemae in the modern era is the emphasis on individuality and self-expression. While tatemae is still vital in formal settings such as business or political interactions, the Japanese people today are more open to expressing their true feelings and opinions, particularly in personal relationships. This is partly due to the influence of Western culture, which places a greater emphasis on individualism and self-expression. In the past, suppressing honne in favor of tatemae was seen as necessary to maintain social harmony and avoid conflict. Many Japanese people today believe honesty and authenticity in personal relationships are essential.

Another significant difference is the role of gender in the use of honne and tatemae. While women were traditionally expected to be more adept at concealing their true feelings and presenting a façade of grace and poise, this has changed somewhat in modern times. Women have gained greater independence and equality, so they are less pressured to conform to traditional gender roles. This has increased the emphasis on honesty and authenticity, particularly in personal relationships.

In the modern era, tatemae is often used to avoid conflict or maintain social harmony. This is particularly true in formal settings such as business or political interactions. However, there is a growing recognition that tatemae can also be used to deceive or manipulate others. Some Japanese people are becoming more skeptical of those who present a façade of politeness or conformity and instead value honesty and authenticity.

A significant difference is technology's role in using honne and tatemae. With the rise of social media and other digital communication tools, people can express their true feelings and opinions more efficiently and to a broader audience. This has led to greater transparency and accountability in many aspects of Japanese society, including politics and business. However, it has also led to a blurring of the boundaries between honne and tatemae, as people can present different faces to different audiences or adopt different personas online.

Despite these changes, honne and tatemae remain essential aspects of Japanese culture in the modern era. They continue to shape social interactions, communication, and personal relationships in unique and nuanced ways. While the emphasis on tatemae has decreased somewhat, it remains an essential aspect of Japanese etiquette and is still valued in many contexts. At the same time, the importance of honne has grown, particularly in personal relationships, as people recognize the value of honesty and authenticity.

The concepts of honne and tatemae have evolved and play a significant role in modern-day Japan. While the emphasis on tatemae has decreased somewhat, it remains an essential aspect of Japanese etiquette and is still valued in many contexts. However, the growing importance of honne reflects a broader cultural shift towards individuality and authenticity. As Japan continues to navigate the challenges of modernity and globalization, the concepts of honne and tatemae will likely remain a crucial part of its cultural identity.

The Hagakure and The Three Masks:

The Hagakure is a text written by Yamamoto Tsunetomo, a samurai from the early 18th century in Japan. It is a compilation of his thoughts and teachings on the samurai way of life. One of the most famous concepts from the Hagakure is the idea of the "three masks."

According to the Hagakure, a samurai should wear three masks: the mask of sincerity, civility, and sincerity and civility combined. These masks are meant to be used in different situations and serve other purposes.

The first mask, the mask of sincerity, is worn when a samurai needs to be honest and straightforward. It is a mask of pure earnestness, where the samurai does not hold back thoughts or feelings. This mask is vital when honesty is valued, such as in a duel or speaking to a superior.

The second mask, the mask of civility, is worn when a samurai needs to show respect and manners. It is a mask of politeness and respect, where the samurai shows deference to others. This mask is essential when social hierarchy and respect for tradition are necessary, such as in a formal ceremony or when interacting with a respected elder.

The third mask, the mask of sincerity and civility combined, is worn when a samurai must balance honesty and civility. It is a mask of harmony, where the samurai seeks to balance openness and respect. This mask is vital when the samurai needs to navigate complex social problems or when dealing with others with different opinions or values.

The concept of the three masks in the Hagakure teaches us that samurai must be able to adapt to different situations and show different sides of themselves depending on the circumstances. By mastering these different masks, samurai can navigate the complexities of the world around them and uphold the values of the samurai way of life.

The three masks in the Hagakure can also be used to understand the relationship between honne and tatemae in Japanese culture.

The first mask, representing the "true face" or honne, can be considered the private self, the innermost thoughts and feelings a person keeps hidden from others. The private thoughts could include personal opinions, desires, and vulnerabilities not typically shared with others.

The second mask, representing the "face shown to others" or tatemae, is the public self-presented to others. This mask is a person's face to the outside world, which may differ from their honne. Tatemae can include social norms and expectations to maintain harmony and avoid conflict in a group or society.

Finally, the third mask, representing the "face used in polite society," can be seen as a combination of honne and tatemae. It is the face presented in formal or polite situations, and it balances the need to express oneself honestly while adhering to societal norms and expectations.

In Japanese culture, it is crucial to be aware of these different expression levels and to navigate them appropriately, depending on the situation. Honne is valued as a way to be true to oneself, but tatemae is vital for maintaining social harmony. The third mask shows that it is possible to strike a balance between the two and that this is often necessary to navigate social situations successfully.

The three masks in the Hagakure can be seen as a visual representation of the relationship between honne and tatemae in Japanese culture. They illustrate the importance of awareness of and navigating these different expression levels to succeed in social interactions.

Chapter Three: Uses and Significance of Honne and Tatemae.

How Honne and Tatemae are Used:

A foreigner might interpret a Japanese person's tatemae as insincere or superficial, leading to misunderstandings or mistrust. Likewise, a Japanese person might feel uncomfortable expressing their honne to someone outside their close circle, which could be seen as breaking social norms. Understanding the context in which honne and tatemae are used is essential.

Tatemae is more likely to be used in formal or public settings, such as in the workplace or with strangers. Honne, on the other hand, is more likely to be expressed in informal or private environments, such as with close friends or family. Moreover, paying attention to nonverbal cues is essential, as these can often convey a person's true feelings even when their words do not. For example, a Japanese person might avoid eye contact or use a more indirect tone when expressing their honne, indicating that they share something personal or sensitive.

Understanding honne and tatemae can be particularly important for building trust and developing relationships in business settings. For instance, a foreign businessperson might need to know the difference between what their Japanese counterpart is saying (tatemae) and what they mean (honne) to make effective decisions and negotiate successfully. Conversely, a Japanese businessperson might need to be aware of how their tatemae is perceived by their foreign counterparts to avoid misunderstandings or miscommunications.

One scenario in which honne and tatemae might be used is in a job interview. The job applicant might present a highly polished and deferential tatemae to the interviewer, emphasizing their qualifications and expressing gratitude for the opportunity to apply for the position. The interviewer might use tatemae to convey a sense of respect and professionalism while also looking for nonverbal cues that indicate the applicant's true feelings or level of interest in the job. Once the formal interview is over, the applicant might express their honne to a trusted friend or family member, revealing their concerns, doubts, and hopes for the position.

Another scenario in which honne and tatemae might be used is in a romantic relationship. At the beginning of the relationship, both partners might use tatemae to convey a sense of politeness and respect while also testing the waters to see how the other person responds. As the relationship progresses, however, they might gradually reveal their honne to each other, expressing their true feelings, desires, and vulnerabilities. At the same time, they might also use tatemae to maintain a sense of harmony and avoid conflicts or hurt feelings.

While the tension between honne and tatemae can create challenges for communication and relationships, understanding these concepts is crucial for anyone seeking to interact with Japanese society on a deeper level. By paying attention to nonverbal cues, contextualizing communication, and striving for authenticity and mutual understanding, it is possible to navigate the complexity of honne and tatemae respectfully and effectively.

How Significant are Honne and Tatemae in Japanese Culture:

A major significance of honne and tatemae is the importance of indirect communication in Japanese culture. Japanese individuals often use tatemae to communicate indirectly because direct contact can be seen as aggressive and rude. Tatemae can be vague language, implied meanings, or nonverbal cues. By using tatemae in this way, individuals can communicate their true intentions without causing offense or discomfort. This emphasis on indirect communication is seen as a way to maintain social harmony and avoid conflict.

Honne and tatemae also have significant implications for relationships in Japanese culture. Building and maintaining relationships is highly valued, and tatemae is often used to show respect and deference to others. For example, individuals may use tatemae to express gratitude, apologize, or show respect to someone in a position of authority. By using tatemae in this way, individuals can maintain positive relationships and demonstrate their commitment to social harmony.

Furthermore, honne and tatemae play a significant role in decision-making in Japanese culture. Decisions are often made through consensus-building, with each group member expressing their tatemae to avoid conflict and maintain harmony. Because consensus is necessary, it can sometimes lead to slower decision-making processes, as everyone must reach an agreement before deciding. However, once a decision is made, everyone is expected to support it fully, even if it goes against their honne. This emphasis on consensus-building is seen as a way to maintain social harmony and avoid conflict.

Another significant aspect of honne and tatemae is their role in the workplace. In Japanese companies, employees are expected to prioritize the goals and interests of the organization over their claims. This expectation is often reinforced through tatemae, where employees may express support for company policies or decisions, even if they disagree. This emphasis on the collective good of the organization is seen as a way to maintain social harmony and ensure the company's success.

Honne and tatemae hold significant cultural significance in Japanese society. They emphasize social harmony, indirect communication, relationship building, consensus-building, and prioritizing the collective good of the organization over personal interests. Understanding the primary significance of these concepts is essential for anyone who wants to interact with Japanese individuals or businesses. By recognizing the role of honne and tatemae in Japanese culture, individuals can navigate social interactions with more sensitivity and respect.

What Role do Honne and Tatemae Play in Social Interactions:

In the workplace, honne and tatemae play a significant role in Japanese society. Employees are expected to follow the rules and procedures set by the company and the group, which is tatemae. For instance, employees are expected to attend meetings and work overtime when necessary, even if they do not agree with the decision or are exhausted. In contrast, honne would be the employee's true feeling and opinion on the issue, which may differ from the group's or company's decision.

This stress can create a conflict between honne and tatemae, and employees may need help to balance the two. For instance, employees may feel uncomfortable with their workload or the pace of the work environment. Still, they are expected to suppress those feelings and show dedication to the company. However, not acknowledging their honne can lead to resentment and dissatisfaction in the workplace.

Honne and tatemae are also important in personal relationships, such as friendships and romantic relationships. In these relationships, tatemae can be used to maintain a positive and harmonious relationship with others. For example, a person may use tatemae by complimenting their friend's outfit or agreeing to plans, even if they dislike the outfit or do not want to go out. Tatemae is used to avoid conflict and maintain harmony in the relationship.

Suppressing one's honne can also lead to misunderstandings and miscommunication in personal relationships. For instance, if someone is not honest about their feelings or opinions, they may unintentionally lead their friend or partner on, creating an unhealthy relationship dynamic.

In public settings, honne and tatemae maintain social norms and etiquette. People in Japan are expected to behave respectfully and politely, which is tatemae. For instance, people are expected to bow when they greet someone, even if they do not particularly like the person or are not in the mood to be polite. The bow is done out of respect and to maintain social harmony.

Not following these social norms can lead to adverse reactions from others. For instance, if someone does not bow to a senior colleague, it may be seen as a sign of disrespect and could harm their professional relationship.

Honne and tatemae can also be seen in personal expressions, such as fashion and art. In Japan, fashion and unique styles express one's individuality and creativity, which is honne. However, there are also social norms and expectations to be followed, which is tatemae. For instance, people are expected to dress conservatively in professional settings, even if they prefer more expressive clothing.

This tension between honne and tatemae can create challenges for individuals who want to express their individuality but also want to fit in and be accepted by society. For instance, people may need to conform to specific fashion trends in their social circle, even if they dislike the movement.

Honne and tatemae are two concepts that are deeply ingrained in Japanese society and culture. While they are often used to maintain social harmony and respect for others, they can also create challenges for individuals who want to express their true feelings and opinions. It is essential to find a balance between honne and tatemae in various social interactions to ensure that honesty and individuality are not sacrificed for social norms and expectations. By being aware of these concepts and understanding how they are used in different situations, individuals can navigate social interactions in Japan with more sensitivity and respect.

What Cultural implications do Honne and Tatemae Have in Japanese Society:

These concepts influence many aspects of social interaction, including communication, relationships, and decision-making. Understanding the cultural implications of honne and tatemae is essential for anyone interested in interacting with Japanese individuals or businesses.

Another cultural implication of honne and tatemae is the importance of indirect communication in Japanese society. Because direct contact can be seen as aggressive and rude, Japanese individuals often use tatemae to communicate indirectly. Tatemae can be vague language, implied meanings, or nonverbal cues. By using tatemae in this way, individuals can express their true intentions without causing offense or discomfort.

Additionally, honne and tatemae also impact decision-making in Japanese society. Decisions are often made through consensus-building, with each group member expressing their tatemae to avoid conflict and maintain harmony. Requiring a consensus can sometimes lead to slower decision-making processes, as everyone must reach an agreement before deciding. However, once a decision is made, everyone is expected to support it fully, even if it goes against their honne.

The cultural implications of honne and tatemae also extend to relationships in Japanese society. Building and maintaining relationships is highly valued, and tatemae is often used to show respect and deference to others. For example, individuals may use tatemae to express gratitude, apologize, or show respect to someone in a position of authority. By using tatemae in this way, individuals can maintain positive relationships and demonstrate their commitment to social harmony.

Honne and tatemae have significant cultural implications in Japanese society and impact social harmony, communication, decision-making, and relationships. Understanding these cultural implications is essential for anyone interested in interacting with Japanese individuals or businesses. By recognizing the role of honne and tatemae in Japanese society, individuals can navigate social interactions with more sensitivity and respect.

Chapter Four: Japanese Concepts That Influence Honne and Tatemae.

Saving Face:

Saving face is a crucial concept in Japanese culture, and it plays a significant role in shaping social interactions and communication patterns. It refers to the desire to maintain one's reputation, avoid embarrassment, and preserve harmony in social interactions. Saving face is closely linked to the Japanese concept of tatemae, which refers to the public face that individuals present to others.

In Japanese culture, maintaining harmony and avoiding conflict are highly valued, and saving face is essential. Individuals are expected to be considerate of others and avoid causing them to feel embarrassed or uncomfortable. In situations where someone has made a mistake or caused an issue, individuals may go to great lengths to minimize the impact of the problem and avoid causing others to lose face.

Saving face is important in Japanese culture because it helps maintain social order and stability. By avoiding conflict and preserving harmony, individuals can maintain positive relationships with others and avoid causing disruptions in social interactions. This is particularly important in Japan, where the concept of Wa, or harmony, is highly valued and essential to maintaining a stable and functioning society.

Another reason saving face is important in Japanese culture is that it helps build trust and respect among individuals. Individuals can build positive relationships and foster trust and respect by showing consideration for others and avoiding causing them to lose face. Saving face is particularly important in business, and professional settings, where maintaining positive relationships is crucial for success.

However, the importance of saving face in Japanese culture can also create challenges for individuals, particularly when expressing their true feelings and opinions. Individuals may feel pressure to conform to group norms and avoid standing out or causing conflict, even if it means suppressing their true feelings or thoughts.

Overall, saving face is a crucial concept in Japanese culture, and it plays a significant role in shaping social interactions and communication patterns. By understanding and navigating this complex system, individuals can effectively communicate and maintain positive relationships with others in Japanese society.

"出る杭伐られる(Deru Kui Atarareru)" "The Tallest Nail Gets Hammered First.":

This Japanese saying suggests that those who stick out, are unique, or excel in a particular way are more likely to be criticized, singled out, or punished for their differences. Just as the tallest nail in a board is the most visible and, therefore, the most vulnerable to being struck down by a hammer, those who are the most noticeable or stand out can be the most susceptible to scrutiny, ridicule, or even oppression.

The saying is often used when conformity is expected, and any deviation from the norm is seen as a potential threat to the status quo. Thus, it is a reminder to be cautious and aware of the consequences of being too different or standing out too much.

The phrase "the tallest nail gets hammered first" reflects the pressure to conform to societal norms, particularly in cultures that value conformity and uniformity. It can also be interpreted as a warning to those considering taking risks or pursuing their passions that they may face criticism, ridicule, or even retribution.

However, it is essential to note that this saying should not be taken as an absolute truth, nor should it be used to discourage individuals from pursuing their dreams or standing up for what they believe in. While it is true that standing out can sometimes bring negative attention, it is also true that some of the most outstanding achievements in history have been made by those who refused to conform and dared to be different.

"The tallest nail gets hammered first" is a warning against standing out too much or being too different, which may result in negative consequences. However, it is essential to remember that this saying is not absolute. Pursuing one's passions and standing up for what one believes in can lead to outstanding achievements and progress.

Indirect Communication:

Indirect communication is a crucial aspect of Japanese culture and plays a significant role in how Japanese people interact. This communication style is known as taido, emphasizing nonverbal communication and subtle hints to convey meaning. Indirect communication is deeply ingrained in Japanese culture and used in various settings, such as business, social, and personal interactions. This chapter will explore how and why indirect communication is essential in Japanese culture.

Indirect communication is essential in Japanese culture because it is seen as a way to maintain harmony and avoid conflict. Direct contact, especially when conveying negative feedback or criticism, can be seen as aggressive and can damage relationships. Through indirect communication, Japanese people can express their thoughts and feelings without causing offense or conflict. For example, instead of saying "no" outright, a Japanese person may use a more indirect response such as "it might be difficult" or "I'll consider it."

Another reason why indirect communication is valued in Japanese culture is because it allows for more nuanced and layered communication. Japanese society strongly emphasizes unspoken messages conveyed through nonverbal cues, such as facial expressions, tone of voice, and body language. These nonverbal cues are often used to describe the speaker's true feelings or intentions, which can be difficult to express through words alone. In this way, indirect communication allows for a more complex and multi-layered conversation that goes beyond the literal meaning of the words.

Indirect communication also plays a role in maintaining social hierarchies in Japanese culture. Japanese society places great importance on social status and rank, reflected in how people interact. In particular, there is a strong expectation that people of higher social levels should be treated with respect and deference. Indirect communication allows for the expression of respect and deference without overtly challenging the social status of the person being addressed. For example, using honorific language or polite forms of address can convey respect and deference without explicitly stating it.

It can also create challenges for those unfamiliar with this communication style. For example, non-Japanese individuals foreign with subtle hints and nonverbal cues may find understanding what is being communicated challenging. This naivety can lead to misunderstandings and miscommunications, damaging relationships and hindering effective communication. Additionally, individuals more accustomed to direct communication may need clarification on indirect contact.

Indirect communication is critical to Japanese culture, and its importance cannot be overstated. It maintains social harmony, facilitates nuanced and layered communication, and reinforces social hierarchies. However, it can also create challenges for those unfamiliar with this communication style. Understanding and appreciating the importance of indirect communication is essential for effective communication and building solid relationships in Japanese culture.

An example is the use of indirect language to express gratitude or apologize. Rather than saying "thank you" directly, a person may use an indirect expression such as "I received your kindness" to express gratitude without causing the other person to feel obligated or indebted. Similarly, when apologizing, individuals may use indirect language such as "I'm sorry that this happened" rather than directly admitting fault to avoid causing the other person to lose face or feel uncomfortable.

Honne and tatemae work with other cultural concepts, such as face-saving and indirect communication, to shape Japanese social interactions and communication patterns. By understanding and navigating these complex systems, individuals can effectively communicate and maintain social harmony in Japanese society.

Mottainai:

Mottainai is a concept deeply rooted in Japanese culture and reflects the importance of resourcefulness and avoiding waste. Mottainai can be seen as a manifestation of both honne and tatemae in Japanese culture, as it reflects both a personal feeling and a social expectation.

On an individual level, the concept of mottainai can be seen as a manifestation of honne or a personal feeling of regret or disappointment in wasting resources. Mottainai can include anything from wasting food to wasting time or energy. Individuals who feel a strong sense of mottainai may be motivated to take action to avoid waste, such as conserving resources or recycling.

Mottainai also reflects a social expectation or tatemae in Japanese culture. In this context, mottainai represents a shared value of resourcefulness and frugality and is an essential aspect of responsible behavior. Avoiding waste is not just a personal choice, but a social expectation reinforced through cultural norms and practices.

Mottainai can be seen as a reflection of the Japanese approach to sustainability and environmentalism. The concept of mottainai emphasizes the importance of reducing waste and making the most of available resources rather than simply consuming and discarding them. In this way, mottainai can be seen as a manifestation of both honne and tatemae, reflecting personal regret and social expectations of responsible behavior.

In addition to its environmental implications, the concept of mottainai also has broader cultural significance. The avoidance of waste can be seen as a reflection of Japanese values of discipline, self-control, and restraint. These values are reflected in various cultural practices, from the art of flower arranging (kado) to the tea ceremony (sado) ritual.

At the same time, the concept of mottainai also reflects the importance of interdependence in Japanese culture. Avoiding waste is not just a personal choice but a social responsibility that requires cooperation and collaboration. In this way, mottainai can be seen as a reflection of the Japanese emphasis on group harmony and social cohesion.

Mottainai represents an essential aspect of Japanese culture, reflecting both personal values and social expectations. The avoidance of waste is seen as a manifestation of both honne and tatemae, reflecting personal feelings of regret and social expectations of responsible behavior. Mottainai can reflect broader cultural values of sustainability, discipline, and interdependence and is an essential aspect of Japanese identity and social norms.

Understanding Failure in Japan:

In Japanese culture, there is a strong emphasis on avoiding failure and maintaining a sense of harmony and balance in all aspects of life. This emphasis on avoiding failure is deeply rooted in the cultural concept of "mottainai," which roughly translates to "what a waste." The idea of mottainai can be seen as a reflection of the traditional Japanese view that resources and opportunities are limited and should be used carefully and efficiently. This concept extends beyond material goods, including social relationships, time, and personal accomplishments.

One of the primary reasons that failure is feared in Japanese culture is that it can lead to a loss of face or reputation. In Japan, maintaining one's reputation is incredibly important. Failure can be seen as a reflection of personal shortcomings or a lack of effort. This feeling can be especially true in business settings, where failure can result in a loss of trust or damage to professional relationships. As a result, many Japanese people are highly motivated to avoid failure and strive for success in all aspects of their lives.

Another reason failure is feared in Japanese culture is that it can have long-term consequences beyond the individual. In a culture that strongly emphasizes social harmony and balance, the failure of one individual can have ripple effects that impact the entire community. For example, if a business fails, it can negatively impact the employees, customers, and suppliers associated with that business. Similarly, a student failing to get into a prestigious school can impact their entire family and community. This emphasis on the interconnectedness of individuals and the impact of individual actions on the broader community can lead to a sense of responsibility and pressure to avoid failure.

In addition to these cultural factors, there are practical reasons why failure is feared in Japan. For example, the Japanese education system strongly emphasizes exams and grades, with students often ranked against one another. This setting can create a highly competitive environment where failure can significantly affect future opportunities and social status. Similarly, the Japanese job market can be highly competitive. Many industries rely on a lifetime employment system where individuals are expected to stay with one company for their careers. In this context, failure to secure a job or advance within a company can impact an individual's career prospects.

Despite the fear of failure in Japanese culture, it is worth noting that failure is not necessarily seen as a permanent condition. Instead, there is a strong belief in the potential for growth and improvement, and failure can be seen as a learning opportunity. This belief is reflected in the Japanese "kaizen" concept, which translates to "continuous improvement." Kaizen emphasizes the importance of minor, incremental improvements over time and encourages individuals to reflect on their failures and make changes to improve their future performance.

The fear of failure in Japanese culture is deeply rooted in the cultural concepts of mottainai, social harmony, and balance. Failure can result in a loss of face, have long-term consequences for the individual and the broader community, and impact future opportunities and social status. However, there is also a belief in the potential for growth and improvement. Failure can be seen as a learning opportunity. By understanding the cultural significance of failure in Japan, individuals can better navigate social interactions and work towards their goals while respecting the values and norms of Japanese society.

Chapter Five: Japanese Social Norms Foreign to the West

Presumption is How the Society Operates:

In Japanese culture, assumptions are often based on a person's actions and interests. A foreigner must know this cultural tendency when interacting with Japanese people. By understanding how inferences are made, a foreigner can take care of how they present themselves to avoid misunderstandings.

Japanese people tend to be observant and pay attention to the actions and interests of others. For example, a person's hobbies or interests can reveal their personality or character. Foreigners should be aware of how they present themselves and what they communicate through their actions and claims. For example, suppose a foreigner is interested in Japanese culture. In that case, it may be assumed that they respect and appreciate the traditions and customs of Japan.

It is also important to note that Japanese people communicate indirectly. Because communication is typically indirect, assumptions are often made based on subtle cues and hints rather than direct statements. A foreigner should pay attention to non-verbal communication, such as tone of voice, facial expressions, and body language, to understand how their actions and interests are perceived.

Another factor to consider is the importance of group harmony in Japanese culture. A foreigner's actions and interests may be seen as disruptive or disrespectful if they go against the group's norms and values. A foreigner must understand their social context and be mindful of how their actions and interests may impact the group.

Suppose a foreigner is in a business meeting with Japanese colleagues. In that case, they should know the group's values and customs. In Japan, punctuality is highly valued, so arriving late to a meeting can be seen as disrespectful. Additionally, it is essential to show respect for the hierarchy within the group by using polite language and deferring to those in positions of authority.

A foreigner's actions and interests may also indicate their personality and character in social situations. For example, suppose a foreigner drinks heavily at a party. In that case, they may be assumed to be irresponsible or lack self-control. On the other hand, if a foreigner expresses interest in traditional Japanese arts such as tea ceremonies or calligraphy, it may be assumed that they are respectful and interested in Japanese culture.

Japanese people tend to make assumptions about others based on their actions and interests, and a foreigner should know this cultural tendency when interacting with Japanese people. By being mindful of how their activities and interests are perceived and understanding their social context, a foreigner can avoid misunderstandings and build positive relationships with Japanese people.

Perception is More Important Than the Truth:

The perception of something is often more important than the truth itself. This focus can be seen in many aspects of life, including personal relationships, business interactions, and social situations. One reason is the emphasis on indirect communication, which can lead to misunderstandings and assumptions based on partial information.

For example, suppose a foreigner meets a Japanese person for the first time and expresses interest in a particular hobby or activity. In that case, the Japanese person may assume that the foreigner is skilled or knowledgeable in that area, even if it is not necessarily true. This assumption may be based on the fact that the foreigner expressed interest in the activity rather than actual evidence of their proficiency. Similarly, suppose a Japanese person meets a foreigner wearing expensive clothing or accessories. In that case, they may assume that the foreigner is wealthy or successful, even if this is not necessarily true.

Often, the perception of something being authentic is more important than reality. The veneer of authenticity is why perception can powerfully influence how people think and behave. For example, suppose a Japanese person believes that a foreigner is knowledgeable or successful. In that case, they may be more likely to seek their advice or assistance. On the other hand, if a Japanese person believes that a foreigner is not skilled or successful, they may be less likely to engage with them in the future.

As a result, foreigners need to be aware of the assumptions that Japanese people may make based on their actions and interests. While it may not be necessary to change one's behavior or appearance entirely, it is crucial to be mindful of how one is perceived and to take steps to ensure that the perception is positive. Positive perception may include being respectful, polite, and considerate in all interactions and being aware of cultural norms and expectations.

Perception of something being accurate is often more important than reality in Japanese culture. This importance can be seen in how Japanese people make assumptions based on partial information and emphasize indirect communication. As a result, it is essential for foreigners to be aware of how they are perceived and to take steps to ensure that the perception is positive, to build strong relationships, and succeed in their interactions with Japanese people.

Ramifications of Failure and Repeated Failure:

Japanese society has a unique perspective on failure and repeated failure, shaped by cultural values such as emphasizing group harmony, personal responsibility, and saving face. Understanding how failure is viewed in Japanese culture is essential for anyone who wants to engage in business or social interactions with Japanese people. This self-study chapter will explore the social ramifications of failure and repeated failure in Japanese culture.

Failure is not simply viewed as an individual shortcoming but also as a reflection of one's social standing and relationships. When an individual fails, it is not just the individual who suffers but also their family and colleagues. Failure can lead to a loss of social status and even ostracism from one's community. Therefore, the stakes for avoiding failure are high in Japanese culture.

In the workplace, failure is a serious issue, and employees are expected to take responsibility for any mistakes. In some cases, failure can lead to demotion or dismissal. The adherence to this cultural norm is because Japanese companies place a high value on efficiency and reliability, and any mistakes or failures can disrupt the smooth functioning of the organization.

Repeated failure can be even more damaging to an individual's social standing than a single failure. It damages one's social status because failure signifies a lack of personal discipline and responsibility. Repeated failures can lead to losing trust and respect from others and even result in social isolation. In Japanese culture, individuals are expected to learn from their mistakes and take steps to improve their performance. Repeated failures can be seen as a failure to understand and improve, a severe character flaw.

In Japanese culture, it is crucial to maintain a positive public image and avoid causing embarrassment or shame to oneself or others. This public image maintenance means that individuals may be reluctant to publicly admit their mistakes or failures for fear of damaging their reputation. Instead, individuals may hide their failures or deflect blame onto others to maintain a positive public image. Hiding your mistakes can make it challenging to address and learn from failures, as individuals may not be willing to acknowledge them publicly.

Failure and repeated failure have significant social ramifications in Japanese culture. Failure is seen as a reflection of one's social standing and relationships, and it can lead to a loss of social status and even ostracism from one's community. Repeated failures are viewed as a lack of personal discipline and responsibility, and they can result in a loss of trust and respect from others. The concept of saving face can also make it difficult for individuals to publicly acknowledge and learn from their failures. Understanding these cultural values is crucial for anyone who wants to engage in business or social interactions with Japanese people.

Chapter Six: Cross-Cultural Communication and Practical Application

Cross-Cultural Communication in Japan:

Cross-cultural communication is an essential aspect of today's globalized world. When communicating across cultures, it is vital to be aware of cultural values, norms, and expectations that can impact how messages are conveyed and received. One important concept to understand in cross-cultural communication is the Japanese concept of honne and tatemae. This self-study chapter will explore why understanding honne and tatemae is important in cross-cultural communication.

The concept of honne and tatemae can help us understand why people from different cultures may say or do things that seem contradictory or insincere. In Japanese culture, it is common for individuals to conceal their true feelings or opinions to maintain social harmony and avoid conflict.

Maintaining social harmony and avoiding conflict can create confusion and misunderstandings for those unfamiliar with this concept. For example, a Japanese person may say yes to a request, even if they do not want to do it, to avoid conflict or show politeness. Someone from another culture may interpret this as a genuine agreement to the request, leading to frustration and confusion when the request still needs to be fulfilled. Understanding the difference between honne and tatemae can help to avoid such misunderstandings in cross-cultural communication.

Another reason why understanding honne and tatemae is essential in cross-cultural communication is that it can help to build trust between individuals from different cultures. When individuals are aware of the cultural differences in communication styles, they can adjust their behavior and style to better align with the other person's expectations.

Suppose a Japanese person is speaking with someone from a culture that values direct communication. In that case, they may need to state their true feelings or opinions to avoid miscommunication explicitly. If the other person recognizes and appreciates this effort, it can build trust and rapport between the two individuals.

Understanding honne and tatemae can also help individuals to respect and appreciate cultural differences. When individuals are aware of the different communication styles and cultural values, they can better recognize and appreciate the unique aspects of other cultures. This awareness helps foster a sense of mutual respect and understanding between individuals from different cultures.

If a Western businessperson negotiates with a Japanese businessperson, understanding the concept of honne and tatemae can help them appreciate the Japanese person's desire to avoid conflict and maintain social harmony. Understanding this cultural norm can help the Western business person to adjust their communication style to better align with the Japanese person's expectations, leading to a more successful negotiation.

While understanding honne and tatemae can benefit cross-cultural communication, it can also be challenging for individuals from cultures that value direct contact. Concealing one's true feelings or opinions can take time to understand or accept for individuals who value honesty and transparency in communication.

Additionally, the concept of honne and tatemae can vary depending on the individual and the situation. For example, an individual may present tatemae in a formal business setting but express honne more openly in a casual social environment. Depending on the case, it can be challenging to know when someone is showing tatemae and when they are telling honne.

Understanding the Japanese concept of honne and tatemae is vital in cross-cultural communication. It can help to avoid misunderstandings, build trust, and foster respect for cultural differences. However, it can also be challenging for individuals from cultures that value direct communication. It is crucial to approach honne and tatemae with an open mind and a willingness to learn and recognize that cultural differences are not inherently good or bad but simply different. Developing a deeper understanding of honne and tatemae can also require patience and a willingness to observe and listen rather than assuming that one's cultural norms are the only valid ones. By taking the time to understand and appreciate these cultural nuances, individuals can build stronger relationships and work more effectively across cultural boundaries.

Practical Application:

Practice Active Listening

When conversing with Japanese people, paying attention to their non-verbal cues is essential. In Japan, non-verbal communication can be as important as verbal communication, revealing much about the other person's thoughts or feelings.

One aspect of non-verbal communication to pay attention to is the tone of voice. In Japan, the tone of someone's voice can communicate much about their emotions, such as whether they are happy, angry, or sad. For example, a person's tone might change when discussing something they are passionate about or upset about. It's essential to listen carefully to the tone of voice of the person you speak with to understand their emotions.

Another important non-verbal cue is facial expressions. In Japan, facial expressions convey many emotions, including happiness, sadness, anger, and surprise. Please pay attention to the other person's facial expressions to get a better idea of how they are feeling. For example, if someone is smiling, they may be happy or amused, but if their eyebrows are furrowed, and their mouth is set in a straight line, they may be upset or angry.

Body language is also an essential aspect of non-verbal communication to pay attention to. In Japan, people may use subtle gestures or postures to communicate their emotions or feelings. For example, someone might nod their head slightly to indicate agreement, or they might cross their arms in front of their body to indicate defensiveness or discomfort. Pay attention to these non-verbal cues to better understand the other person's feelings.

By paying attention to non-verbal cues, you can better understand the other person's thoughts and feelings, even if their words don't match. Non-verbal cues can be critical when navigating sensitive or delicate topics, such as discussing differences in opinion or addressing potential conflicts.

Non-verbal cues are a critical aspect of communicating effectively with Japanese people. By listening carefully to the tone of voice, facial expressions, and body language of the person you speak with, you can better understand their emotions and feelings. These tools can help you to communicate more effectively and avoid misunderstandings.

Avoid Direct Confrontation

In Japanese culture, confrontation is often considered impolite and can cause discomfort. Instead, approaching sensitive topics indirectly or through subtle hints is preferred. This cultural norm of avoiding confrontation is deeply ingrained in Japanese society and is rooted in maintaining social harmony and avoiding conflict.

As a foreigner conversing with a Japanese person, it is essential to be mindful of this cultural norm and to respect it. Confrontation can be interpreted as a sign of disrespect and can damage relationships. When communicating with Japanese people, it is crucial to approach sensitive topics with tact and diplomacy.

One way to avoid confrontation is to use indirect language or to approach the topic through subtle hints. For example, instead of asking someone directly if they are upset, you can ask if everything is okay or if there is anything you can do to help. This approach allows the person to express their feelings without feeling pressured to do so directly.

Another strategy for avoiding confrontation is to use non-verbal cues, such as tone of voice, facial expressions, and body language, to convey your message. By carefully choosing your words and being mindful of your non-verbal cues, you can communicate your message without causing discomfort or offense.

It is also important to note that indirect language and subtle hints can effectively communicate in many situations, not just those sensitive. In Japanese culture, communication is often more implicit and nuanced than in other cultures, which can also be reflected in everyday conversations.

Avoiding confrontation is an essential aspect of communication in Japanese culture. By using indirect language, approaching topics through subtle hints, and being mindful of non-verbal cues, you can effectively communicate with Japanese people while maintaining social harmony and avoiding misunderstandings. As a foreigner conversing with a Japanese person, it is essential to be aware of this cultural norm and to respect it to build strong relationships and communicate effectively.

Respect Hierarchy

When it comes to communicating with Japanese people, respecting hierarchy is essential. In Japanese culture, status and age play an important role in how people interact with each other and show respect to those who are older or of higher social status than you are highly valued. Here are some practical tips for respecting hierarchy in Japanese culture:

Using polite language is a crucial way to show respect in Japanese culture. Politeness is highly valued, and using formal language when speaking with people you do not know well or those older or of higher status is essential. There are different levels of politeness in Japanese, with the most formal language used in formal situations or when speaking with someone of very high status.

In Japan, people are often referred to by their title rather than their name, especially in formal situations. It is vital to use the appropriate title when addressing someone, such as "sensei" for a teacher, "sama" for someone of high status, or "san" for someone who is neither a close friend nor of very high social status.

Honorifics, or suffixes added to a person's name or title, are also crucial in Japanese communication. Using the appropriate honorific shows respect and acknowledges the other person's status. For example, adding "sama" or "san" to someone's name or title is a common honorific in Japanese.

Bowing is a common sign of respect in Japanese culture, especially in formal situations. When meeting someone for the first time, it is customary to bow slightly. The depth of the bow depends on the case and the status of the person you are greeting. Generally, the deeper the bow, the higher the respect shown.

Listening respectfully is also an essential aspect of showing respect in Japanese culture. When someone of higher status speaks, listening attentively and showing that you are engaged in the conversation is vital. Nodding and eye contact is critical nonverbal cues showing respect and engagement.

Understanding hierarchy is an essential part of communicating effectively in Japanese culture. By using polite language, appropriate titles, honorifics, bowing as a sign of respect, and listening respectfully, you can show respect to those older or of higher status than you. Following these suggestions helps maintain social harmony, fosters positive relationships, and avoids misunderstandings.

Avoid Blunt Language

As a foreigner conversing with a Japanese person, it is essential to understand that Japanese culture values indirect and subtle communication. Blunt language can be seen as aggressive and rude, leading to misunderstandings and discomfort. Here are some reasons why avoiding straightforward language is vital in Japanese communication:

Japanese culture places a strong emphasis on maintaining social harmony and avoiding conflict. Using blunt language can disrupt this harmony and create tension in relationships. By utilizing softer language and expressions, you can convey your message while still maintaining a polite and respectful tone.

Respect for others is a crucial value in Japanese culture. Using blunt language can be seen as disrespectful and rude, especially when speaking with those who are older or of higher status. By using polite language and avoiding confrontation, you can show respect for others and their opinions.

We discussed saving face as an essential concept in Japanese culture, which means avoiding embarrassment or causing someone else to lose face. Using blunt language can embarrass or offend someone, causing the person to lose face in front of others. You can avoid causing someone to lose face and maintain positive relationships by using indirect speech and softening your message.

Using blunt language may be acceptable in some cultures, but it is not the norm in Japanese culture. By utilizing softer language and expressions, you can adapt to the cultural norms of Japan and show that you understand and respect their communication style.

Blunt language can lead to misunderstandings and confusion, especially when communicating across cultures. By using indirect speech and paying attention to non-verbal cues, you can better understand the true meaning behind someone's words and avoid misinterpreting their message.

Avoiding blunt language is essential in Japanese communication because it helps maintain social harmony, shows respect for others, saves face, adapts to cultural norms, and avoids misunderstandings. As a foreigner conversing with a Japanese person, it is vital to be aware of these cultural values and communicate in a way that is respectful and considerate of the other person. By using indirect language and paying attention to non-verbal cues, you can effectively communicate with Japanese people and build positive relationships.

Practice Active Listening

Active listening is essential to communication in any culture, but it is especially crucial in Japan. Japanese culture places great value on interpersonal harmony, and active listening is one way to show respect and understanding toward the person you are communicating with. Here are some practical tips on how to practice active listening when conversing with Japanese people:

When communicating with a Japanese person, please give them your full attention. Full attention means avoiding distractions like looking at your phone or checking your surroundings. Instead, focus on the speaker and maintain eye contact to show you are actively listening.

Nodding your head and using other encouraging gestures such as smiling, nodding along, and leaning forward can help show the speaker that you are engaged in the conversation and interested in what they say. These non-verbal cues encourage the speaker to continue and feel more comfortable sharing their thoughts and opinions.

In Japanese culture, interrupting the speaker can be seen as impolite and disrespectful. It is vital to allow the speaker to finish what they are saying before responding. Patiently taking turns speaking shows that you are listening to and respecting their opinions.

To show that you genuinely understand the speaker, try paraphrasing them or repeating what they said in your own words. This technique helps clarify misunderstandings and shows that you are trying to understand the speaker's perspective fully.

Asking follow-up questions is a great way to show you are actively listening and interested in the conversation. Follow-up questions demonstrate that you are engaged in the conversation and want to learn more about the speaker's thoughts and opinions.

Finally, it is essential to show empathy and understanding toward the speaker. Even if you disagree with their perspective, acknowledging their feelings and showing that you understand where they are coming from can help to maintain social harmony and avoid misunderstandings.

Practicing active listening is a crucial aspect of communication in Japanese culture. By giving the speaker your full attention, using encouraging gestures, avoiding interruptions, paraphrasing and repeating back, asking follow-up questions, and showing empathy and understanding, you can effectively communicate with Japanese people while showing respect and maintaining social harmony.

Following these practical tips for applying Honne and Tatemae, you can effectively communicate with Japanese people while maintaining social harmony and avoiding misunderstandings. It is important to remember that Honne and Tatemae are not fixed concepts but rather dynamic aspects of Japanese culture that can change depending on the situation and the person you are speaking with. Therefore, it is vital to approach each conversation with an open mind and a willingness to adapt to the social norms of Japanese culture.

Chapter Seven: Recognizing Honne and Tatemae with Tips and Strategies

Recognizing and Responding to Honne and Tatemae:

Recognizing when honne and tatemae are used can be challenging, but some tips can help. One of the critical ways to acknowledge honne and tatemae is by paying attention to non-verbal cues such as body language, tone of voice, and facial expressions. Japanese people often use indirect speech to avoid conflict, and it is essential to understand the underlying message being conveyed.

If a Japanese person is using tatemae, it is often best to follow suit and respond in a way that maintains social harmony. Responding with directness or bluntness can offend and damage the relationship. It is also vital to avoid confronting the person and instead find a more subtle way to communicate your true feelings or thoughts. This more subtle way can be accomplished by using indirect language or implying your intentions through your actions.

In contrast, when a Japanese person uses honne, listening carefully and responding thoughtfully to their honne is crucial. Honne often reveals a person's genuine emotions and feelings. Answering with sensitivity and understanding can help build trust and rapport. Suppose a Japanese person shares their honne with you. In that case, it is essential to maintain their confidentiality and not share their feelings with others.

It is also essential to avoid making assumptions or judgments based on honne and tatemae. While honne is a person's true thoughts and feelings, acting on them in social situations is not always appropriate. Tatemae is used to maintain social harmony, but it does not necessarily mean the person is insincere or dishonest. Understanding the balance between honne and tatemae can take time and practice. Still, it is essential to build solid relationships in Japanese culture.

When conversing with a Japanese person, it is essential to recognize when honne and tatemae are being used and respond accordingly. Paying attention to non-verbal cues, using indirect language, and avoiding confrontation is critical for navigating these concepts. Responding thoughtfully to honne and respecting the balance between honne and tatemae can help build trust and rapport in Japanese culture. With practice and awareness, foreigners can communicate effectively with Japanese people and build meaningful relationships.

Tips and Tricks for Recognizing Honne and Tatemae:

As a foreigner conversing with Japanese people, it can take time to understand their communication style, which relies heavily on the concepts of honne and tatemae. One way to recognize honne is by paying attention to nonverbal cues. Japanese people express their true feelings through subtle nonverbal signals, such as facial expressions and body language. For example, if a Japanese person is smiling, but their eyes are not, it could indicate that their honne does not match their tatemae.

Another way to recognize honne is to listen carefully to what is not being said. Japanese people often communicate indirectly and may not say what they mean outright. Instead, they may use vague language, speak in euphemisms, or rely on context to convey their true feelings. Therefore, paying attention to the underlying meaning of what is being said is crucial.

Recognizing tatemae can be more challenging since it requires understanding social norms and cultural context. One way to identify tatemae is to observe how Japanese people interact with others. For example, using formal language and gestures when speaking with a superior could indicate tatemae.

Another way to recognize tatemae is by paying attention to the situation. Japanese people may adjust their behavior depending on the setting and the people they are with. For example, in a formal business setting, they may be more reserved and use formal language. In contrast, in a casual environment with friends, they may be more relaxed and use informal language.

Understanding the social norms and cultural context can help identify tatemae. Learn about Japanese culture and etiquette to better understand how to behave in different situations.

Be patient and respectful as Japanese people may only sometimes express their honne outright, and it can take time to build trust and rapport. It's essential to be patient and respectful in all interactions.

Understanding the concepts of honne and tatemae is crucial to effectively communicating with Japanese people. By paying attention to nonverbal cues, listening carefully, and understanding the context, it's possible to recognize these concepts and build better relationships with Japanese colleagues, friends, and acquaintances.

Strategies and Situations with "honne" and "tatemae":

As a foreigner conversing with Japanese people, navigating these concepts and understanding what is genuinely meant in a conversation can be challenging. In this chapter, we will explore three examples of situations where honne and tatemae come into play and how a foreigner should respond.

Example 1: Giving and Receiving Compliments

In Japan, giving and receiving compliments is a complex social ritual often involving honne and tatemae. When someone gets praise, they are expected to downplay their achievements and express humility, even if they are proud. Downplaying their achievements is an example of tatemae. However, it is essential to understand that the person receiving the compliment may genuinely feel proud of their accomplishments, an instance of honne.

When giving a compliment, it is best to keep it modest and avoid exaggerating. When receiving praise, it is important to express gratitude and humility, even if you are proud of your accomplishments. However, expressing genuine appreciation for the compliment is also acceptable while maintaining a sense of humility.

Example 2: Disagreeing with Others

In Japanese culture, open disagreement is often considered impolite and aggressive, creating challenges for foreigners who are used to expressing their opinions freely. Instead of openly disagreeing, it is common for Japanese people to use indirect language or make suggestions rather than give direct answers. Suggesting an alternative in question format is an example of tatemae.

Be mindful of the cultural norms around saving face when expressing disagreement. Instead of openly disagreeing, it is best to use indirect language and make suggestions rather than giving a direct answer. Paying attention to non-verbal cues such as facial expressions and tone of voice is essential, which can provide insight into a person's true feelings.

Example 3: Invitations and Refusals

In Japan, it is common to make indirect invitations, such as suggesting that someone might enjoy visiting a particular place, rather than directly inviting them. Similarly, when refusing an invitation, it is common to provide an indirect response rather than a direct "no." Giving an excuse for a scheduled event at the same time as your invitation is an example of tatemae.

When receiving an indirect invitation, it is best to take the suggestion as an invitation and express interest rather than wait for a direct invitation.

When refusing an invitation, it is best to use indirect language and express regret rather than giving an immediate "no."

Example 4: Job Interviews

Job interviews in Japan can be a challenging experience for foreigners, as they often involve a significant amount of tatemae. During a job interview, it is common for the interviewer to ask indirect questions or make suggestions rather than give a direct answer. The indirect questions and suggestions gauge the candidate's social awareness and ability to read between the lines.

While interviewing for a job in Japan, it is crucial to be mindful of these cultural norms and respond appropriately. When answering questions, it is best to use indirect language and make suggestions rather than giving a direct answer. Paying attention to non-verbal cues such as facial expressions and tone of voice is essential, which can provide insight into the interviewer's true feelings. By being aware of these cultural norms and responding appropriately, a foreigner can demonstrate their social awareness and increase their chances of success in a job interview.

Example 5: Business Meetings

In Japan, business meetings often involve significant tatemae, as it is considered impolite to disagree with a superior or colleague openly. Instead of openly opposing, it is common for Japanese people to use indirect language or make suggestions rather than give direct answers. An idea that doesn't challenge a proposal is made to maintain harmony within the group and avoid confrontational situations.

When expressing disagreement, it is best to use indirect language and make suggestions rather than giving a direct answer. Paying attention to non-verbal cues such as facial expressions and tone of voice is essential, which can provide insight into a person's true feelings. By being mindful of these cultural norms and responding appropriately, a foreigner can demonstrate their respect for Japanese culture and build strong business relationships.

Example 6: Social Events

In Japan, social events often involve a significant amount of tatemae, as it is considered impolite to be too direct or open about one's feelings. When receiving an invitation to a social event, it is common for Japanese people to provide an indirect response rather than a direct "yes" or "no."

Declining due to engagements is done to maintain social harmony and avoid offending.

When receiving an invitation, it is best to take the suggestion as an invitation and express interest rather than wait for a direct invitation. When declining an invitation, it is best to use indirect language and express regret rather than giving a curt "no." Paying attention to non-verbal cues such as facial expressions and tone of voice is essential, which can provide insight into a person's true feelings. By being mindful of these cultural norms and responding appropriately, a foreigner can demonstrate their respect for Japanese culture and build strong social relationships.

Navigating honne and tatemae in conversations with Japanese people can be challenging for foreigners. Still, by developing active listening skills, reading non-verbal cues, and being aware of cultural norms, it is possible to create strong relationships and communicate effectively. By understanding these concepts and responding appropriately in various situations, foreigners can navigate the complexities of Japanese culture and build solid and lasting relationships.

Conclusion

Congratulations on finishing " *Cracking the Code: Honne and Tatemae in Japan*." Throughout the book, we have explored the basics of these concepts, their historical context, contemporary examples, and cultural implications.

Understanding "honne" and "tatemae" in Japanese society is crucial, as they are deeply ingrained in Japanese culture and social interactions. They play a vital role in maintaining relationships and social harmony. This book has shown that understanding these concepts is essential for anyone navigating Japanese society and engaging in cross-cultural communication.

The historical context section traced the development of "honne" and "tatemae" over time and how cultural influences have shaped them. The contemporary examples section emphasized the differences between how these concepts are used today compared to the past and their role in social interactions.

The cultural implications section discussed the significance of "honne" and "tatemae" in Japanese culture and how they relate to other cultural concepts such as face-saving and indirect communication. It highlighted the importance of understanding these concepts when interacting with Japanese people and different cultures and how they can impact communication and relationships.

The practical applications section offered tips and strategies for foreigners interacting with Japanese people. It explained how to recognize and respond to "honne" and "tatemae," providing strategies for navigating situations where they come into play.

I hope I have comprehensively explained the Japanese concepts of "honne" and "tatemae," their cultural implications, and their practical applications. Understanding these concepts allows readers to navigate Japanese society more effectively and confidently engage in cross-cultural communication. Remember to keep an open mind, be respectful, and practice patience when interacting with Japanese people. Best of luck in your cross-cultural communication endeavors!

About the Author

Meet Brian Takahashi, a teacher/writer immersed in Japanese culture for over a decade. As a current teacher and proud husband to a Japanese wife (whom he swears is his better half), he's had plenty of opportunities to observe the subtle differences between honne and tatemae in action.

You can find him typing at his keyboard, sipping on green tea, and dreaming up new stories in his spare time. He's been known to sneak in a few pages during period breaks (don't tell his students!), but he's also happy to discuss the finer points of Japanese literature and culture over a cold beer.

With a degree in Asian Language and Literature, he's well-equipped to navigate the nuances of Japanese culture, but he's constantly learning and expanding his knowledge. Whether exploring new parts of Japan with his family or diving into a new book, he's always close to his trusty laptop.

So please sit back, grab a cup of tea, and get ready to delve into the world of honne and tatemae with a writer who knows the culture inside and out (or at least thinks he does).